STARK LIBRARY

Dinosaurs

Ankylosaurus

by Julie Murray

Dash!
LEVELED READERS
An Imprint of Abdo Zoom • abdobooks.com

Dash!
LEVELED READERS

Level 1 – Beginning
Short and simple sentences with familiar words or patterns for children who are beginning to understand how letters and sounds go together.

Level 2 – Emerging
Longer words and sentences with more complex language patterns for readers who are practicing common words and letter sounds.

Level 3 – Transitional
More developed language and vocabulary for readers who are becoming more independent.

THIS BOOK CONTAINS RECYCLED MATERIALS

abdobooks.com

Published by Abdo Zoom, a division of ABDO, PO Box 398166, Minneapolis, Minnesota 55439. Copyright © 2023 by Abdo Consulting Group, Inc. International copyrights reserved in all countries. No part of this book may be reproduced in any form without written permission from the publisher. Dash!™ is a trademark and logo of Abdo Zoom.

Printed in the United States of America, North Mankato, Minnesota.
052022
092022

Photo Credits: Alamy, Getty Images, Shutterstock
Production Contributors: Kenny Abdo, Jennie Forsberg, Grace Hansen, John Hansen
Design Contributors: Candice Keimig, Neil Klinepier

Library of Congress Control Number: 2021950316

Publisher's Cataloging in Publication Data

Names: Murray, Julie, author.
Title: Ankylosaurus / by Julie Murray
Description: Minneapolis, Minnesota : Abdo Zoom, 2023 | Series: Dinosaurs | Includes online resources and index.
Identifiers: ISBN 9781098228262 (lib. bdg.) | ISBN 9781098229108 (ebook) | ISBN 9781098229528 (Read-to-Me ebook)
Subjects: LCSH: Ankylosaurus--Juvenile literature. | Dinosaurs--Juvenile literature. | Paleontology--Juvenile literature. | Extinct animals--Juvenile literature.
Classification: DDC 567.90--dc23

Table of Contents

Ankylosaurus 4

More Facts 22

Glossary 23

Index 24

Online Resources 24

Ankylosaurus

Ankylosaurus lived 70 million years ago. It was an **ankylosaurid** dinosaur.

It lived in places with warm **climates** and lots of plants.

It was 20 feet (6.1 m) long. It stood 6 feet (1.8 m) tall. It weighed 12,000 pounds (5,443 kg).

Ankylosaurus walked on four legs. Its legs were short and strong.

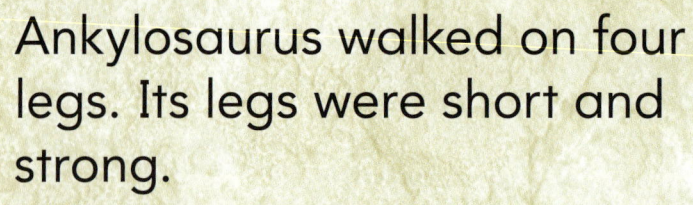

Ankylosaurus was protected by the hard, bony plates that covered its body.

It had a long, clubbed tail.
Its tail was used for defense.

Ankylosaurus was a plant-eater. It ate low-lying plants.

The first Ankylosaurus **fossils** were found in Montana in 1906.

Other **fossils** have been found in Wyoming. Some were also discovered in Alberta, Canada.

More Facts

- *Ankylosaurus* means "**fused** lizard."

- It moved slowly. Its top speed was 8 miles per hour (12.9 kph).

- Ankylosaurus **fossils** are rare. The dinosaur may have preferred living upland, away from rivers. River bottoms are good places for fossils to form.

Glossary

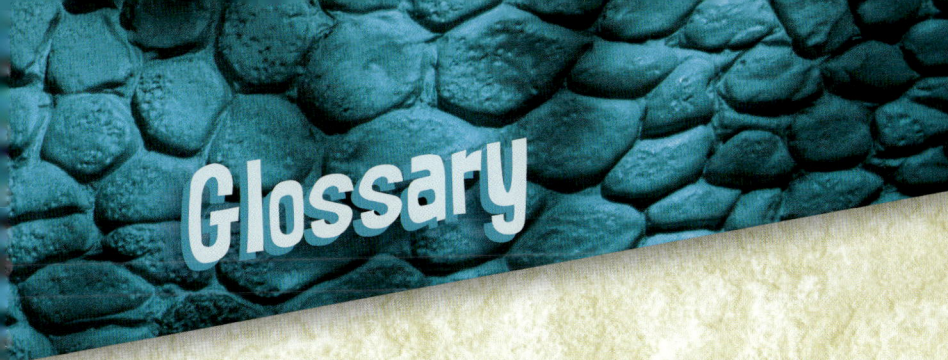

ankylosaurid – an armored dinosaur of a group whose members are typically plant-eaters, four-legged, heavily armored and tank-like.

climate – the usual weather conditions in a place.

fossil – the remains or trace of a living animal or plant from a long time ago. Fossils are found embedded in earth or rock.

fused – joined to form a single entity.

Index

Alberta, Canada 20

defense 12, 14

food 16

fossils 19, 20

habitat 7

legs 10

Montana, USA 19, 20

plates 12

size 9

tail 14

weight 9

Wyoming, USA 20

Online Resources

Booklinks
NONFICTION NETWORK
FREE! ONLINE NONFICTION RESOURCES

To learn more about Ankylosaurus, please visit **abdobooklinks.com** or scan this QR code. These links are routinely monitored and updated to provide the most current information available.